Country Captain Chicken Cookbook

Discover the Authentic Flavors of Country Captain Chicken

COUNTRY CAPTAIN CHICKEN COOKBOOK

First edition. January 22, 2024.

ISBN: 979-8224130597

Written by Sammy Andrews.

Table of Contents

Sammy Andrews

Chapter 1: Introduction to Country Captain Chicken

Welcome to the flavorful world of Country Captain Chicken! In this chapter, we'll take a journey back in time to explore the historical origins and culinary significance of this classic dish. From its humble beginnings to its esteemed place in various traditions, Country Captain Chicken has woven itself into the tapestry of global cuisine.

Historical Origins

The roots of Country Captain Chicken can be traced back to Southern kitchens, where it was first crafted as a fusion of Indian and American flavors. The dish got its name from British sea captains who, having experienced the rich culinary landscape of India, brought the recipe back to the American South. Over the years, it evolved, adapted, and became a cherished classic.

Significance in Culinary Traditions

What makes Country Captain Chicken special is not just its taste, but the cultural significance it carries. This dish is a symbol of blending diverse culinary influences, creating a harmonious fusion that speaks to the crossroads of history. It has been a centerpiece in family gatherings, celebrations, and community feasts, passing down from generation to generation.

As we embark on this culinary journey, you'll discover the unique elements that make Country Captain Chicken a beloved dish in various regions. From its aromatic spices to the way it brings people together, there's a rich tapestry of stories woven into every bite.

Whether you're a seasoned chef or a kitchen novice, this cookbook is your guide to mastering the art of Country Captain Chicken. Get ready to explore its variations, experiment with spices, and create memorable meals that honor tradition while embracing modern creativity.

In the following chapters, we'll dive into the heart of Country Captain Chicken, exploring classic recipes, regional twists, and innovative adaptations. So, grab your apron, sharpen those knives, and let's embark on a culinary adventure that celebrates the timeless allure of Country Captain Chicken.

Chapter 2: Classic Country Captain Chicken Recipe

In this chapter, we'll dive into the heart of Country Captain Chicken with a timeless classic recipe. From the essential ingredients to the step-by-step cooking instructions, you'll master the art of creating a dish that pays homage to its rich history.

Ingredients and Preparation

Ingredients:

- 1 whole chicken, cut into pieces
- 2 tablespoons vegetable oil
- 1 large onion, finely chopped
- 3 cloves garlic, minced
- 1 bell pepper, diced
- 1 cup tomatoes, chopped
- 2 tablespoons curry powder
- 1 teaspoon ground cumin
- 1 teaspoon paprika
- 1/2 teaspoon cayenne pepper (adjust to taste)
- Salt and black pepper to taste
- 1 cup chicken broth
- 1/2 cup raisins
- 1/2 cup slivered almonds, toasted
- Fresh cilantro, chopped (for garnish)
- Cooked rice (for serving)

Preparation:

Marination:

- Season chicken pieces with salt, black pepper, and 1 tablespoon of curry powder.

- Let it marinate for at least 30 minutes, allowing the flavors to infuse.

Toasting Almonds:

- In a dry skillet over medium heat, toast slivered almonds until golden brown. Set aside for later use.

Cooking Process:

- In a large skillet or Dutch oven, heat vegetable oil over medium-high heat.
- Add marinated chicken pieces and brown them on all sides. Remove from the skillet and set aside.

Aromatics:

- In the same skillet, add chopped onions, garlic, and bell pepper. Sauté until softened.

Spice Infusion:

- Add remaining curry powder, ground cumin, paprika, and cayenne pepper. Stir well to coat the aromatics with the spices.

Tomatoes and Broth:

- Incorporate chopped tomatoes into the mixture. Cook until they break down and release their juices.
- Pour in chicken broth, deglazing the pan and creating a flavorful base.

Return of the Chicken:

- Place the browned chicken pieces back into the skillet. Ensure each piece is coated with the aromatic mixture.

Simmer and Infuse:

- Cover and simmer over low heat for 30-40 minutes, allowing the chicken to absorb the flavors.

Final Touch:

- Stir in raisins and toasted almonds. Adjust seasoning if needed.

Garnish and Serve:

- Sprinkle fresh cilantro over the dish.
- Serve the Country Captain Chicken over a bed of cooked rice.

Now, you've created a classic Country Captain Chicken dish that's not only delicious but also a testament to the culinary fusion that makes this recipe timeless. Enjoy the rich flavors and aromatic spices that define this beloved dish!

Chapter 3: Regional Variations

Country Captain Chicken has taken on diverse forms as it traveled across different regions. In this chapter, we'll explore three distinct variations—Southern Style, Northern Twists, and International Influences—each adding a unique touch to this classic dish.

3.1 Southern Style

Ingredients and Preparation:

- Emphasis on aromatic spices like cayenne, thyme, and bay leaves
- Use of locally sourced tomatoes and bell peppers
- Incorporation of okra for a Southern twist
- Serve with classic cornbread or biscuits

Cooking Instructions:

- Follow the classic recipe for Country Captain Chicken with an emphasis on Southern flavors.
- Add a handful of sliced okra to the skillet when sautéing the aromatics.
- Consider using smoked paprika for a hint of smokiness.
- Serve the Southern Style Country Captain Chicken over a bed of grits or with classic Southern sides like collard greens.

3.2 Northern Twists

Ingredients and Preparation:

- Subtle use of spices with a focus on herbs like thyme and rosemary
- Incorporation of root vegetables like carrots and potatoes
- Use of apple cider or white wine for a Northern touch

- Serve with crusty bread or mashed potatoes

Cooking Instructions:

- Begin with the classic recipe but reduce the intensity of cayenne pepper for a milder flavor.
- Add diced carrots and potatoes to the skillet when sautéing the aromatics.
- Instead of raisins, consider adding dried cranberries for a Northern sweetness.
- Finish the dish with a splash of apple cider or white wine before simmering.
- Serve the Northern Twists Country Captain Chicken with crusty bread or mashed potatoes.

3.3 International Influences

Ingredients and Preparation:

- Experiment with global spices like garam masala, turmeric, or za'atar
- Use coconut milk for a tropical twist
- Incorporate ingredients like pineapple, mango, or olives for international flair
- Serve with couscous, naan, or plantains, depending on the influence

Cooking Instructions:

- Infuse global flavors by replacing some traditional spices with those commonly used in international cuisine.
- Substitute a portion of the chicken broth with coconut milk for a creamy texture.
- Experiment with additional ingredients like pineapple chunks, mango slices, or olives during the cooking process.

- Consider serving the International Influences Country Captain Chicken with couscous, naan bread, or fried plantains.

Exploring these regional variations will allow you to appreciate the versatility of Country Captain Chicken and its ability to adapt to different culinary traditions. Choose the variation that intrigues your taste buds and transports you to a culinary journey around the world!

Chapter 4: The Spice Rack: A Guide to Essential Ingredients

In this chapter, we'll explore the magical world of spices, herbs, and aromatics that elevate Country Captain Chicken to a symphony of flavors. From must-have spices to the vibrant freshness of herbs, let's delve into the essentials that make this dish truly exceptional.

4.1 Must-Have Spices

4.1.1 Curry Powder:

A blend of coriander, cumin, turmeric, and other spices, curry powder is the star of the show. Choose a high-quality blend or experiment with your own ratios to find the perfect balance for your taste.

4.1.2 Cumin:

With its warm, earthy flavor, cumin adds depth to the dish. Toasting cumin seeds before grinding them enhances their aroma and intensifies the flavor.

4.1.3 Paprika:

Whether it's sweet, smoked, or hot, paprika contributes a rich color and a hint of sweetness or smokiness to the dish. Choose the type that complements your preferred flavor profile.

4.1.4 Cayenne Pepper:

For those who enjoy a bit of heat, cayenne pepper is the go-to spice. Adjust the quantity to your spice preference, balancing heat with the other flavors.

4.1.5 Coriander:

Ground coriander or freshly crushed coriander seeds add citrusy and slightly sweet notes, enhancing the overall complexity of the spice blend.

4.1.6 Black Pepper:

Freshly ground black pepper adds a pungent kick and enhances the overall spiciness of the dish. Don't shy away from using it liberally.

4.1.7 Salt:

A crucial element in any dish, salt not only seasons the chicken but also enhances the other flavors. Use it judiciously, tasting as you go.

4.2 Fresh Herbs and Aromatics

4.2.1 Garlic:

Minced or crushed garlic infuses the dish with a robust, savory flavor. Adjust the quantity based on your love for garlic.

4.2.2 Onion:

Finely chopped onions form the flavor base of the dish. Experiment with different varieties like sweet onions or red onions for subtle variations.

4.2.3 Bell Pepper:

Diced bell peppers add a sweet and crunchy texture. Choose red, green, or yellow peppers to add a burst of color and flavor.

4.2.4 Cilantro:

Fresh cilantro leaves, chopped just before serving, add a burst of freshness. If you're not a cilantro fan, consider using parsley as an alternative.

4.2.5 Thyme:

Dried or fresh thyme contributes earthiness and a subtle herby note. Use it sparingly, as it can be potent.

4.2.6 Bay Leaves:

A couple of bay leaves during simmering add a subtle aromatic background. Remember to remove them before serving.

4.2.7 Ginger:

Grated or minced ginger provides a zesty warmth to the dish. Adjust the quantity based on your preference for ginger's spiciness.

Armed with this guide to essential ingredients, you're ready to create a Country Captain Chicken that sings with the harmonious balance of spices and the vibrant freshness of herbs. Experiment with quantities, trust your palate, and make this dish truly your own.

Chapter 5: Mastering the Art of Marination

In this chapter, we'll explore the transformative process of marination, where flavors meld and chicken becomes a canvas for culinary art. From traditional marination techniques that pay homage to the roots of Country Captain Chicken to creative marinades that add a modern twist, this chapter will guide you in mastering this essential step.

5.1 Traditional Marination Techniques

5.1.1 Yogurt-Based Marinade:

Inspired by Indian culinary traditions, a yogurt-based marinade tenderizes the chicken while infusing it with a rich, tangy flavor. Combine yogurt with spices like cumin, coriander, and a touch of turmeric for an authentic experience.

5.1.2 Buttermilk Soak:

A Southern classic, a buttermilk soak not only imparts a subtle tanginess but also helps to tenderize the chicken. Season the buttermilk with salt, pepper, and a dash of hot sauce for an extra kick.

5.1.3 Dry Rub:

For a quicker marination process, a dry rub is a go-to technique. Coat the chicken with a blend of your favorite spices, salt, and a touch of brown sugar for caramelization during cooking.

5.1.4 Citrus Infusion:

Bring a burst of freshness with a citrus marinade. Combine lemon or lime juice with zest, garlic, and herbs for a bright and zesty flavor that complements the warm spices of Country Captain Chicken.

5.1.5 Oil-Based Marinade:

Create a flavor-packed base with an oil-based marinade. Mix olive oil or vegetable oil with crushed garlic, herbs, and a dash of vinegar for a Mediterranean-inspired twist.

5.2 Creative Marinades

5.2.1 Tropical Paradise:

Transport your taste buds to the tropics with a marinade featuring coconut milk, pineapple juice, and a hint of rum. Add a touch of curry powder and cayenne for a Caribbean-inspired infusion.

5.2.2 Smoky Mesquite:

Channel the flavors of the American South with a smoky mesquite marinade. Combine smoked paprika, cumin, and a touch of liquid smoke for a barbecue-inspired experience.

5.2.3 Honey Mustard Elegance:

Elevate your dish with a sweet and savory honey mustard marinade. Mix Dijon mustard, honey, garlic, and a splash of white wine for a sophisticated twist.

5.2.4 Asian Fusion:

Infuse Asian flavors with a soy-based marinade. Combine soy sauce, ginger, sesame oil, and a touch of Sriracha for a savory and slightly spicy profile.

5.2.5 Herb Garden Delight:

Celebrate the freshness of herbs with a garden-inspired marinade. Blend fresh basil, parsley, thyme, and rosemary with olive oil for a fragrant and herbaceous infusion.

Experiment with these traditional and creative marination techniques to discover the perfect flavor profile that suits your palate. Whether you're drawn to the comforting familiarity of traditional methods or the exciting innovation of creative marinades, the art of marination is a key step in creating a memorable Country Captain Chicken dish.

Chapter 6: Perfecting Rice Accompaniments

In this chapter, we'll delve into the art of crafting the perfect rice accompaniments for your Country Captain Chicken. From the classic elegance of Pilaf to exploring creative rice alternatives, these sides are designed to complement and elevate the overall dining experience.

6.1 Pilaf Perfection

6.1.1 Classic Basmati Pilaf

Ingredients:

- 1 cup Basmati rice
- 2 tablespoons vegetable oil or ghee
- 1 onion, finely chopped
- 2 cloves garlic, minced
- 1 teaspoon cumin seeds
- 2 cups chicken or vegetable broth
- Salt and pepper to taste

Instructions:

1. Rinse the Basmati rice under cold water until the water runs clear.
2. In a pot, heat oil or ghee over medium heat. Add cumin seeds and sauté until fragrant.
3. Add chopped onions and garlic, sautéing until golden brown.
4. Stir in the Basmati rice, coating it in the aromatic mixture.
5. Pour in the chicken or vegetable broth, season with salt and pepper, and bring to a boil.
6. Reduce heat to low, cover, and simmer for 15-20 minutes or until the rice is cooked and the liquid is absorbed.
7. Fluff the rice with a fork, and your Classic Basmati Pilaf is ready

to serve.

6.1.2 Almond and Raisin Pilaf
Ingredients:

- 1 cup Basmati rice
- 2 tablespoons vegetable oil or ghee
- 1/2 cup slivered almonds, toasted
- 1/2 cup raisins
- 1 onion, finely chopped
- 2 cloves garlic, minced
- 1 teaspoon cumin seeds
- 2 cups chicken or vegetable broth
- Salt and pepper to taste

Instructions:

1. Follow the instructions for Classic Basmati Pilaf.
2. During the sautéing of onions and garlic, add toasted slivered almonds and raisins to the mixture.
3. Continue with the remaining steps, creating a delightful Almond and Raisin Pilaf.

6.1.3 Lemon Herb Pilaf
Ingredients:

- 1 cup Basmati rice
- 2 tablespoons vegetable oil or ghee
- Zest of 1 lemon
- 2 tablespoons fresh parsley, chopped
- 1 teaspoon fresh thyme leaves
- 1 onion, finely chopped

- 2 cloves garlic, minced
- 1 teaspoon cumin seeds
- 2 cups chicken or vegetable broth
- Salt and pepper to taste

Instructions:

1. Follow the instructions for Classic Basmati Pilaf.
2. During the sautéing of onions and garlic, add lemon zest, chopped parsley, and fresh thyme to the mixture.
3. Continue with the remaining steps, creating a vibrant Lemon Herb Pilaf.

6.1.4 Coconut Jasmine Pilaf
Ingredients:

- 1 cup Jasmine rice
- 1 cup coconut milk
- 1/2 cup shredded coconut
- 2 tablespoons vegetable oil
- 1 onion, finely chopped
- 2 cloves garlic, minced
- 1 teaspoon cumin seeds
- Salt and pepper to taste

Instructions:

1. Rinse the Jasmine rice under cold water until the water runs clear.
2. In a pot, heat oil over medium heat. Add cumin seeds and sauté until fragrant.
3. Add chopped onions and garlic, sautéing until golden brown.
4. Stir in the Jasmine rice, coating it in the aromatic mixture.
5. Pour in coconut milk, add shredded coconut, season with salt and pepper, and bring to a boil.
6. Reduce heat to low, cover, and simmer for 15-20 minutes or until the rice is cooked and the liquid is absorbed.
7. Fluff the rice with a fork, and your Coconut Jasmine Pilaf is ready to serve.

6.2 Rice Alternatives

6.2.1 Cauliflower Rice

Ingredients:

- 1 head of cauliflower, grated or processed into rice-sized pieces
- 2 tablespoons vegetable oil
- 1 onion, finely chopped
- 2 cloves garlic, minced
- 1 teaspoon cumin
- Salt and pepper to taste

Instructions:

1. In a large skillet, heat oil over medium heat.
2. Add chopped onions and garlic, sautéing until translucent.
3. Add cauliflower rice, cumin, salt, and pepper, stirring to combine.
4. Cook for 5-7 minutes until the cauliflower is tender but not mushy.
5. Serve your Country Captain Chicken over this low-carb Cauliflower Rice alternative.

6.2.2 Quinoa Blend

Ingredients:

- 1 cup quinoa, rinsed
- 2 cups chicken or vegetable broth
- 1 cup diced vegetables (bell peppers, carrots, peas)
- 2 tablespoons fresh herbs (parsley, cilantro), chopped
- 1 tablespoon olive oil
- Salt and pepper to taste

Instructions:

1. In a pot, combine quinoa and broth, bringing it to a boil.
2. Reduce heat, cover, and simmer for 15 minutes.
3. In a separate pan, sauté diced vegetables in olive oil until tender.
4. Combine cooked quinoa, sautéed vegetables, and fresh herbs.
5. Fluff with a fork, season with salt and pepper, and serve alongside your Country Captain Chicken.

6.2.3 Couscous Medley

Ingredients:

- 1 cup couscous
- 1 cup cherry tomatoes, halved
- 1 cucumber, diced
- 2 tablespoons fresh mint, chopped
- 2 tablespoons fresh parsley, chopped
- 1 tablespoon olive oil
- Salt and pepper to taste

Instructions:

1. Prepare couscous according to package instructions.
2. In a large bowl, combine cooked couscous, cherry tomatoes, cucumber, mint, parsley, and olive oil.
3. Toss gently until well mixed.
4. Season with salt and pepper to taste, and serve this refreshing Couscous Medley with your Country Captain Chicken.

6.2.4 Wild Rice Pilaf
Ingredients:

- 1 cup wild rice blend (wild rice and brown rice)
- 2 cups chicken or vegetable broth
- 1 cup mushrooms, sliced
- 1 shallot, finely chopped
- 2 tablespoons white wine
- 2 tablespoons olive oil
- Salt and pepper to taste

Instructions:

1. In a pot, combine the wild rice blend and broth. Bring to a boil, then reduce heat and simmer for 45 minutes or until rice is tender.
2. In a skillet, sauté mushrooms and shallots in olive oil until softened.
3. Deglaze the pan with white wine, scraping up any browned bits.
4. Combine the cooked wild rice with the mushroom mixture.
5. Season with salt and pepper, and serve this hearty Wild Rice Pilaf with your Country Captain Chicken.

Whether you opt for the classic elegance of Pilaf or experiment with these rice alternatives, these sides will complement your Country Captain Chicken, providing a well-rounded and satisfying dining experience. Enjoy the interplay of textures and flavors as you perfect the art of pairing rice with this beloved dish.

Chapter 7: One-Pot Wonders

In this chapter, we'll explore the convenience and flavor-packed goodness of one-pot wonders featuring Country Captain Chicken. From quick and easy weeknight recipes to slow-cooked delights that simmer to perfection, these dishes are designed to make your cooking experience enjoyable and the dining experience unforgettable.

7.1 Easy Weeknight Recipes

7.1.1 Quick and Spicy Chicken Skillet

Ingredients:

- 1 pound boneless, skinless chicken thighs, cut into bite-sized pieces
- 2 tablespoons vegetable oil
- 1 onion, diced
- 2 cloves garlic, minced
- 1 bell pepper, sliced
- 1 cup cherry tomatoes, halved
- 2 tablespoons Country Captain Chicken spice blend
- 1 cup chicken broth
- 1 cup quick-cooking rice
- Salt and pepper to taste
- Fresh cilantro for garnish

Instructions:

1. In a large skillet, heat oil over medium-high heat.
2. Add chicken pieces and brown on all sides.
3. Add diced onion and minced garlic, sauté until softened.
4. Stir in bell pepper, cherry tomatoes, and Country Captain Chicken spice blend.

5. Pour in chicken broth and bring to a simmer.
6. Add quick-cooking rice, cover, and cook for 10-15 minutes or until the rice is tender.
7. Season with salt and pepper to taste.
8. Garnish with fresh cilantro and serve directly from the skillet.

7.1.2 30-Minute Country Captain Pasta

Ingredients:

- 1 pound penne pasta
- 2 tablespoons olive oil
- 1 pound boneless, skinless chicken breasts, thinly sliced
- 1 onion, finely chopped
- 3 cloves garlic, minced
- 1 can (14 oz) diced tomatoes
- 2 tablespoons Country Captain Chicken spice blend
- 1 cup chicken broth
- Salt and pepper to taste
- Grated Parmesan cheese for serving

Instructions:

1. Cook the penne pasta according to package instructions.
2. In a large skillet, heat olive oil over medium heat.
3. Add sliced chicken and cook until browned.
4. Add chopped onion and minced garlic, sauté until fragrant.
5. Pour in diced tomatoes, Country Captain Chicken spice blend, and chicken broth.
6. Simmer for 10-15 minutes until the sauce thickens.
7. Season with salt and pepper.
8. Serve the Country Captain Chicken sauce over cooked penne pasta.

9. Garnish with grated Parmesan cheese.

7.2 Slow-Cooked Delights
7.2.1 Crockpot Country Captain Stew
Ingredients:

- 2 pounds bone-in, skin-on chicken thighs
- 1 large onion, sliced
- 3 cloves garlic, minced
- 1 bell pepper, chopped
- 2 tablespoons Country Captain Chicken spice blend
- 1 can (14 oz) crushed tomatoes
- 1 cup chicken broth
- 1 cup long-grain rice
- Salt and pepper to taste
- Chopped fresh parsley for garnish

Instructions:

1. In a slow cooker, layer chicken thighs, sliced onion, minced garlic, and chopped bell pepper.
2. Sprinkle Country Captain Chicken spice blend over the ingredients.
3. Pour in crushed tomatoes and chicken broth.
4. Cover and cook on low for 4-6 hours until chicken is tender.
5. Stir in long-grain rice, cover, and cook for an additional 30 minutes or until the rice is cooked.
6. Season with salt and pepper.
7. Garnish with chopped fresh parsley before serving.

7.2.2 Braised Country Captain Chicken Thighs
Ingredients:

- 4 bone-in, skin-on chicken thighs

- 2 tablespoons vegetable oil
- 1 onion, finely chopped
- 2 cloves garlic, minced
- 1 cup diced tomatoes
- 2 tablespoons Country Captain Chicken spice blend
- 1 cup chicken broth
- 1 cup jasmine rice
- Salt and pepper to taste
- Chopped green onions for garnish

Instructions:

1. In a large, oven-safe skillet, heat oil over medium-high heat.
2. Season chicken thighs with Country Captain Chicken spice blend, salt, and pepper.
3. Brown chicken thighs on both sides and set aside.
4. In the same skillet, sauté chopped onion and minced garlic until softened.
5. Add diced tomatoes, chicken broth, and jasmine rice. Stir to combine.
6. Nestle the browned chicken thighs into the rice mixture.
7. Cover and transfer the skillet to a preheated oven at 375°F (190°C).
8. Bake for 30-40 minutes or until the chicken is cooked through and the rice is tender.
9. Garnish with chopped green onions before serving.

Whether you're pressed for time on a weeknight or looking to savor the slow-cooked flavors on a lazy weekend, these one-pot wonders provide a range of options for incorporating Country Captain Chicken into your meals.

Chapter 8: Grilled and Roasted Creations

In this chapter, we'll explore the delightful world of grilled and roasted Country Captain Chicken creations. From outdoor cooking adventures with smoky flavors from the grill to oven-baked marvels that infuse the dish with aromatic warmth, these recipes are sure to elevate your Country Captain Chicken experience.

8.1 Outdoor Cooking Adventures

8.1.1 Smoky Grilled Country Captain Drumsticks

Ingredients:

- 8 chicken drumsticks
- 3 tablespoons vegetable oil
- 2 tablespoons Country Captain Chicken spice blend
- 1 tablespoon smoked paprika
- 1 teaspoon cayenne pepper
- 1/4 cup honey
- Salt and pepper to taste
- Lemon wedges for serving

Instructions:

1. In a bowl, mix vegetable oil, Country Captain Chicken spice blend, smoked paprika, cayenne pepper, honey, salt, and pepper.
2. Coat the drumsticks with the marinade, ensuring they are well covered. Marinate for at least 1 hour.
3. Preheat the grill to medium-high heat.
4. Grill the drumsticks for 20-25 minutes, turning occasionally, until cooked through and slightly charred.
5. Baste with additional honey during the last 5 minutes of cooking.
6. Serve with lemon wedges for a burst of freshness.

8.1.2 Grilled Country Captain Vegetable Skewers
Ingredients:

- 1 pound boneless, skinless chicken thighs, cut into chunks
- 1 zucchini, sliced
- 1 red bell pepper, diced
- 1 red onion, cut into wedges
- 2 tablespoons olive oil
- 2 tablespoons Country Captain Chicken spice blend
- Salt and pepper to taste
- Wooden skewers, soaked in water

Instructions:

1. In a bowl, combine chicken chunks, zucchini slices, red bell pepper, and red onion.
2. Drizzle olive oil over the mixture and sprinkle with Country Captain Chicken spice blend, salt, and pepper. Toss to coat evenly.
3. Thread the marinated chicken and vegetables onto soaked wooden skewers.
4. Preheat the grill to medium heat.
5. Grill the skewers for 15-20 minutes, turning occasionally, until the chicken is cooked through and the vegetables are tender.
6. Serve the grilled skewers over a bed of rice or couscous.

8.2 Oven-Baked Marvels
8.2.1 Roasted Country Captain Chicken Thighs
Ingredients:

- 4 bone-in, skin-on chicken thighs
- 2 tablespoons olive oil
- 2 tablespoons Country Captain Chicken spice blend
- 1 tablespoon honey

- 1 lemon, sliced
- Salt and pepper to taste
- Fresh parsley for garnish

Instructions:

1. Preheat the oven to 375°F (190°C).
2. Rub chicken thighs with olive oil, Country Captain Chicken spice blend, honey, salt, and pepper.
3. Place the chicken thighs on a baking sheet lined with parchment paper.
4. Arrange lemon slices around the chicken.
5. Roast in the oven for 30-35 minutes or until the chicken reaches an internal temperature of 165°F (74°C).
6. Garnish with fresh parsley before serving.

8.2.2 Baked Country Captain Chicken Casserole

Ingredients:

- 2 pounds boneless, skinless chicken breasts, cut into cubes
- 1 cup jasmine rice
- 1 onion, finely chopped
- 2 cloves garlic, minced
- 1 cup diced tomatoes
- 2 tablespoons Country Captain Chicken spice blend
- 2 cups chicken broth
- 1/2 cup raisins
- 1/2 cup slivered almonds
- Fresh cilantro for garnish

Instructions:

1. Preheat the oven to 375°F (190°C).
2. In a large baking dish, combine chicken cubes, jasmine rice, chopped onion, minced garlic, diced tomatoes, and Country Captain Chicken spice blend.
3. Pour chicken broth over the mixture and stir to combine.
4. Cover the baking dish with foil and bake for 30 minutes.
5. Remove the foil, stir in raisins and slivered almonds, and bake uncovered for an additional 15-20 minutes or until the rice is cooked, and the chicken is tender.
6. Garnish with fresh cilantro before serving.

Chapter 9: Sauces and Sides

In this chapter, we'll delve into the world of sauces that amplify the flavor of Country Captain Chicken, as well as explore a variety of complementary side dishes that will enhance your dining experience.

9.1 Flavorful Sauces

9.1.1 Spiced Tomato Chutney

Ingredients:

- 1 cup diced tomatoes
- 1/2 cup red onion, finely chopped
- 2 cloves garlic, minced
- 1 teaspoon grated ginger
- 1 tablespoon Country Captain Chicken spice blend
- 2 tablespoons brown sugar
- 1/4 cup apple cider vinegar
- Salt to taste
- Fresh cilantro, chopped, for garnish

Instructions:

1. In a saucepan, combine diced tomatoes, red onion, garlic, ginger, Country Captain Chicken spice blend, brown sugar, and apple cider vinegar.
2. Simmer over medium heat, stirring occasionally, until the chutney thickens, about 15-20 minutes.
3. Season with salt to taste.
4. Allow the chutney to cool before serving.
5. Garnish with fresh cilantro before serving alongside Country Captain Chicken.

9.1.2 Yogurt Mint Sauce

Ingredients:

- 1 cup Greek yogurt
- 1/4 cup fresh mint, finely chopped
- 1 teaspoon cumin
- 1 clove garlic, minced
- Salt and pepper to taste
- Lemon juice to taste

Instructions:

1. In a bowl, combine Greek yogurt, chopped mint, cumin, minced garlic, salt, pepper, and a splash of lemon juice.
2. Stir until well combined.
3. Adjust the seasoning and lemon juice to taste.
4. Refrigerate for at least 30 minutes before serving.
5. Serve this refreshing yogurt mint sauce alongside grilled Country Captain Chicken.

9.2 Complementary Side Dishes
9.2.1 Garlic Naan Bread
Ingredients:

- 2 cups all-purpose flour
- 1 teaspoon baking powder
- 1/2 teaspoon baking soda
- 1/4 teaspoon salt
- 1 cup plain yogurt
- 2 tablespoons ghee or melted butter
- 2 cloves garlic, minced
- Fresh cilantro, chopped, for garnish

Instructions:

1. In a bowl, whisk together flour, baking powder, baking soda, and salt.
2. Add yogurt and mix until a dough forms.
3. Knead the dough on a floured surface until smooth.
4. Divide the dough into small balls and roll each into a thin oval shape.
5. Heat a skillet over medium heat.
6. Cook each naan for 1-2 minutes on each side until puffed and lightly browned.
7. Mix melted butter or ghee with minced garlic.
8. Brush the garlic butter mixture over the warm naan.
9. Garnish with chopped cilantro before serving.

9.2.2 Turmeric Roasted Vegetables
Ingredients:

- 2 cups mixed vegetables (carrots, broccoli, cauliflower)

- 2 tablespoons olive oil
- 1 teaspoon turmeric
- 1/2 teaspoon cumin
- Salt and pepper to taste
- Lemon wedges for serving

Instructions:

1. Preheat the oven to 400°F (200°C).
2. In a bowl, toss mixed vegetables with olive oil, turmeric, cumin, salt, and pepper.
3. Spread the vegetables on a baking sheet in a single layer.
4. Roast in the oven for 20-25 minutes or until the vegetables are golden and tender.
5. Squeeze lemon juice over the roasted vegetables before serving.

9.2.3 Coconut Cilantro Rice
Ingredients:

- 1 cup basmati rice
- 1 cup coconut milk
- 1 cup water
- 1/4 cup fresh cilantro, chopped
- Salt to taste
- 1 tablespoon shredded coconut for garnish

Instructions:

1. Rinse the basmati rice under cold water until the water runs clear.
2. In a pot, combine rice, coconut milk, water, and salt.
3. Bring to a boil, then reduce heat, cover, and simmer for 15-20 minutes or until the rice is cooked.
4. Fluff the rice with a fork and stir in chopped cilantro.

5. Garnish with shredded coconut before serving.

Explore the world of sauces that add depth to Country Captain Chicken and discover a variety of side dishes that complement its rich flavors.

Chapter 10: Country Captain Chicken Salads

In this chapter, we'll explore the world of vibrant and refreshing salads featuring the flavorful Country Captain Chicken. From fresh and crisp salad creations to unique dressings that perfectly complement the richness of the dish, these recipes will add a delightful twist to your culinary repertoire.

10.1 Fresh and Vibrant Salad Creations

10.1.1 Mango Avocado Country Captain Chicken Salad

Ingredients:

- 2 cups cooked and shredded Country Captain Chicken
- 2 cups mixed salad greens
- 1 ripe mango, peeled and diced
- 1 avocado, sliced
- 1/4 cup red onion, thinly sliced
- 1/4 cup cherry tomatoes, halved
- 1/4 cup cucumber, sliced
- 1/4 cup fresh cilantro, chopped
- 1/4 cup feta cheese, crumbled

Instructions:

1. In a large bowl, combine shredded Country Captain Chicken, mixed salad greens, diced mango, sliced avocado, red onion, cherry tomatoes, cucumber, and chopped cilantro.
2. Toss the salad gently to mix the ingredients.
3. Sprinkle crumbled feta cheese over the top.
4. Serve immediately, and consider drizzling with your favorite dressing.

10.1.2 Grilled Peach and Arugula Country Captain Chicken Salad

Ingredients:

- 2 cups cooked and shredded Country Captain Chicken
- 4 cups arugula
- 2 peaches, halved and grilled
- 1/4 cup goat cheese, crumbled
- 1/4 cup pecans, toasted
- Balsamic vinaigrette dressing

Instructions:

1. Grill halved peaches until caramelized marks appear.
2. In a large salad bowl, combine shredded Country Captain Chicken, arugula, grilled peaches, crumbled goat cheese, and toasted pecans.
3. Toss the salad gently.
4. Drizzle with balsamic vinaigrette dressing just before serving.

10.2 Unique Dressings
10.2.1 Curry Yogurt Dressing
Ingredients:

- 1/2 cup Greek yogurt
- 1 teaspoon curry powder
- 1 tablespoon honey
- 1 tablespoon Dijon mustard
- Salt and pepper to taste

Instructions:

1. In a bowl, whisk together Greek yogurt, curry powder, honey, Dijon mustard, salt, and pepper.
2. Adjust the seasoning to taste.
3. Use as a dressing for your Country Captain Chicken salads.

10.2.2 Citrus Cilantro Vinaigrette
Ingredients:

- Juice of 1 orange
- Juice of 1 lime
- 1/4 cup fresh cilantro, chopped
- 2 tablespoons olive oil
- 1 teaspoon honey
- Salt and pepper to taste

Instructions:

1. In a small bowl, combine orange juice, lime juice, chopped cilantro, olive oil, honey, salt, and pepper.
2. Whisk until well combined.
3. Drizzle over your favorite Country Captain Chicken salad for a burst of citrusy freshness.

Feel free to get creative and mix and match ingredients to create your own signature Country Captain Chicken salads.

Chapter 11: Hearty Soups and Stews

In this chapter, we'll explore the comforting world of hearty soups and stews featuring the nourishing goodness of Country Captain Chicken. These recipes are designed to warm your soul and provide a cozy and satisfying dining experience.

11.1 Classic Country Captain Chicken Soup
Ingredients:

- 2 cups cooked and shredded Country Captain Chicken
- 1 tablespoon olive oil
- 1 onion, finely chopped
- 2 carrots, diced
- 2 celery stalks, sliced
- 3 cloves garlic, minced
- 1 teaspoon Country Captain Chicken spice blend
- 6 cups chicken broth
- 1 cup diced tomatoes
- 1 cup spinach, chopped
- Salt and pepper to taste
- Cooked rice for serving
- Fresh parsley for garnish

Instructions:

1. In a large pot, heat olive oil over medium heat.
2. Add chopped onion, carrots, celery, and minced garlic. Sauté until vegetables are softened.
3. Sprinkle Country Captain Chicken spice blend over the vegetables and stir to coat.
4. Pour in chicken broth and bring to a simmer.
5. Add diced tomatoes and shredded Country Captain Chicken.

Simmer for 15-20 minutes.

6. Stir in chopped spinach and cook until wilted.
7. Season with salt and pepper to taste.
8. Serve the soup over cooked rice, garnished with fresh parsley.

11.2 Slow-Cooked Country Captain Chicken Stew

Ingredients:

- 2 pounds bone-in, skin-on chicken thighs
- 1 tablespoon vegetable oil
- 1 onion, finely chopped
- 3 cloves garlic, minced
- 1 bell pepper, diced
- 2 carrots, sliced
- 2 potatoes, diced
- 2 tablespoons Country Captain Chicken spice blend
- 1 can (14 oz) crushed tomatoes
- 4 cups chicken broth
- Salt and pepper to taste
- Fresh cilantro for garnish

Instructions:

1. In a large skillet, heat vegetable oil over medium-high heat.
2. Season chicken thighs with salt and pepper, then brown them on both sides in the skillet. Set aside.
3. In the same skillet, sauté chopped onion, minced garlic, bell pepper, carrots, and potatoes until softened.
4. Sprinkle Country Captain Chicken spice blend over the vegetables and stir to coat.
5. Transfer the browned chicken and sautéed vegetables to a slow cooker.

6. Add crushed tomatoes and chicken broth.
7. Cover and cook on low for 6-8 hours or until the chicken is tender and falls off the bone.
8. Before serving, shred the chicken and stir it back into the stew.
9. Season with salt and pepper to taste.
10. Garnish with fresh cilantro before serving.

These hearty soups and stews offer a comforting bowl of nourishment, perfect for warming up on chilly days or providing a hearty and satisfying meal. Enjoy the robust flavors and heartwarming aromas that these Country Captain Chicken creations bring to your table.

Chapter 12: Fusion Fare: Country Captain Chicken Beyond Borders

In this chapter, we'll embark on a culinary journey that transcends borders, exploring international fusion recipes that infuse the rich flavors of Country Captain Chicken with diverse and exotic culinary influences.

12.1 Thai-Inspired Country Captain Chicken Curry

Ingredients:

- 2 cups cooked and shredded Country Captain Chicken
- 1 tablespoon red curry paste
- 1 can (14 oz) coconut milk
- 1 cup bamboo shoots, sliced
- 1 cup bell peppers, sliced
- 1 tablespoon fish sauce
- 1 tablespoon brown sugar
- Fresh cilantro for garnish
- Cooked jasmine rice for serving

Instructions:

1. In a large skillet, simmer red curry paste in coconut milk over medium heat until fragrant.
2. Add shredded Country Captain Chicken, bamboo shoots, and bell peppers to the skillet.
3. Stir in fish sauce and brown sugar, allowing the flavors to meld.
4. Simmer for 10-15 minutes until the curry thickens and vegetables are tender.
5. Garnish with fresh cilantro and serve over jasmine rice.

12.2 Mexican-Inspired Country Captain Chicken Tacos

Ingredients:

- 2 cups cooked and shredded Country Captain Chicken
- 8 small flour or corn tortillas
- 1 cup black beans, drained and rinsed
- 1 cup corn kernels
- 1 cup cherry tomatoes, diced
- 1 cup red cabbage, shredded
- 1 avocado, sliced
- Lime wedges for serving
- Fresh cilantro for garnish

Instructions:

1. Warm tortillas in a dry skillet or microwave.
2. Fill each tortilla with shredded Country Captain Chicken, black beans, corn, cherry tomatoes, red cabbage, and avocado slices.
3. Squeeze lime over the filling.
4. Garnish with fresh cilantro before serving.

12.3 Mediterranean-Inspired Country Captain Chicken Pita Wrap

Ingredients:

- 2 cups cooked and shredded Country Captain Chicken
- 4 whole wheat pita bread
- 1 cup Greek yogurt
- 1 cucumber, diced
- 1 cup cherry tomatoes, halved
- 1/2 cup Kalamata olives, sliced
- 1/4 cup red onion, finely chopped
- Fresh mint for garnish

Instructions:

1. In a bowl, combine shredded Country Captain Chicken, diced cucumber, cherry tomatoes, Kalamata olives, and red onion.
2. Warm the pita bread.
3. Spread a spoonful of Greek yogurt on each pita.
4. Fill with the Country Captain Chicken mixture.
5. Garnish with fresh mint before serving.

12.4 Japanese-Inspired Country Captain Chicken Sushi Bowl
Ingredients:

- 2 cups cooked and shredded Country Captain Chicken
- 2 cups sushi rice, cooked
- 1 cup edamame, shelled
- 1/2 cup carrots, julienned
- 1/2 cup cucumber, sliced
- 1 avocado, sliced
- Nori strips for garnish
- Sesame seeds for garnish
- Soy sauce for drizzling

Instructions:

1. In a bowl, arrange sushi rice, shredded Country Captain Chicken, edamame, carrots, cucumber, and avocado slices.
2. Garnish with nori strips and sesame seeds.
3. Drizzle with soy sauce before serving.

Embark on a global fusion adventure with these international-inspired Country Captain Chicken recipes. From the vibrant flavors of Thai curry to the zesty goodness of Mexican tacos, these fusion dishes bring together the best of both worlds for a truly unique and delicious dining experience. Enjoy the fusion fare that takes Country Captain Chicken beyond borders!

Chapter 13: Family Gatherings and Feasts

In this chapter, we'll focus on recipes perfect for family gatherings and feasts, offering large batch options and crowd-pleasing variations of Country Captain Chicken that will make your celebrations memorable.

13.1 Classic Country Captain Chicken Casserole

Ingredients:

- 4 pounds bone-in, skin-on chicken thighs
- 2 tablespoons vegetable oil
- 2 onions, finely chopped
- 4 cloves garlic, minced
- 2 bell peppers, diced
- 4 tablespoons Country Captain Chicken spice blend
- 4 cups long-grain rice
- 2 cans (28 oz each) crushed tomatoes
- 6 cups chicken broth
- Salt and pepper to taste
- Chopped fresh parsley for garnish

Instructions:

1. In a large, oven-safe casserole dish, heat vegetable oil over medium-high heat.
2. Season chicken thighs with Country Captain Chicken spice blend, salt, and pepper.
3. Brown chicken thighs on both sides in the casserole dish.
4. Add chopped onions, minced garlic, and diced bell peppers. Sauté until softened.
5. Stir in long-grain rice, crushed tomatoes, and chicken broth.
6. Cover and transfer the casserole dish to a preheated oven at 375°F (190°C).

7. Bake for 45-50 minutes or until the chicken is cooked through, and the rice is tender.
8. Garnish with chopped fresh parsley before serving.

13.2 Country Captain Chicken Sliders
Ingredients:

- 4 cups cooked and shredded Country Captain Chicken
- 12 slider buns
- 1 cup coleslaw
- 1/2 cup pickles, sliced
- 1/2 cup mayonnaise
- 2 tablespoons Dijon mustard
- Salt and pepper to taste

Instructions:

1. In a large bowl, combine shredded Country Captain Chicken, mayonnaise, Dijon mustard, salt, and pepper.
2. Mix until well combined.
3. Toast the slider buns.
4. Spoon the Country Captain Chicken mixture onto the bottom half of each bun.
5. Top with coleslaw and sliced pickles.
6. Place the other half of the bun on top to create sliders.
7. Serve these crowd-pleasing Country Captain Chicken sliders at your family gatherings.

13.3 Country Captain Chicken Chili
Ingredients:

- 3 pounds ground chicken
- 2 tablespoons vegetable oil
- 2 onions, finely chopped

- 4 cloves garlic, minced
- 3 bell peppers, diced
- 1/4 cup chili powder
- 2 tablespoons Country Captain Chicken spice blend
- 2 cans (14 oz each) diced tomatoes
- 2 cans (15 oz each) black beans, drained and rinsed
- 2 cans (15 oz each) kidney beans, drained and rinsed
- 4 cups chicken broth
- Salt and pepper to taste
- Shredded cheddar cheese and sour cream for topping

Instructions:

1. In a large pot, heat vegetable oil over medium-high heat.
2. Add ground chicken, chopped onions, minced garlic, and diced bell peppers. Cook until chicken is browned.
3. Sprinkle chili powder and Country Captain Chicken spice blend over the chicken mixture. Stir to combine.
4. Pour in diced tomatoes, black beans, kidney beans, and chicken broth.
5. Bring to a simmer and cook for 30-40 minutes, allowing the flavors to meld.
6. Season with salt and pepper to taste.
7. Serve the Country Captain Chicken chili topped with shredded cheddar cheese and a dollop of sour cream.

These large batch recipes and crowd-pleasing variations of Country Captain Chicken are perfect for family gatherings and feasts.

Chapter 14: Healthy Twists on Country Captain Chicken

In this chapter, we'll explore healthy and nutritious versions of Country Captain Chicken, featuring light and wholesome ingredients, as well as dietary modifications to cater to various health-conscious preferences.

14.1 Grilled Country Captain Chicken Salad
Ingredients:

- 2 cups cooked and shredded Country Captain Chicken
- 6 cups mixed salad greens
- 1 cup cherry tomatoes, halved
- 1 cucumber, sliced
- 1/4 cup red onion, thinly sliced
- 1/4 cup feta cheese, crumbled
- Balsamic vinaigrette dressing

Instructions:

1. In a large bowl, combine shredded Country Captain Chicken, mixed salad greens, cherry tomatoes, cucumber, red onion, and crumbled feta cheese.
2. Toss the salad gently.
3. Drizzle with balsamic vinaigrette dressing just before serving.

14.2 Country Captain Chicken Lettuce Wraps
Ingredients:

- 2 cups cooked and shredded Country Captain Chicken
- Large lettuce leaves (such as iceberg or butter lettuce)
- 1 cup quinoa, cooked

- 1 cup broccoli slaw
- 1/4 cup almonds, sliced
- Greek yogurt sauce (Greek yogurt, lemon juice, garlic, salt)

Instructions:

1. Fill each lettuce leaf with a spoonful of shredded Country Captain Chicken, cooked quinoa, broccoli slaw, and sliced almonds.
2. Drizzle with Greek yogurt sauce before serving.

14.3 Cauliflower Rice Country Captain Bowl
Ingredients:

- 2 cups cooked and shredded Country Captain Chicken
- 4 cups cauliflower rice
- 1 cup peas
- 1/2 cup carrots, finely diced
- 1/4 cup raisins
- Fresh cilantro for garnish

Instructions:

1. In a large skillet, sauté cauliflower rice, peas, and diced carrots until tender.
2. Stir in shredded Country Captain Chicken and raisins.
3. Cook until everything is heated through.
4. Garnish with fresh cilantro before serving.

14.4 Gluten-Free Country Captain Chicken Quinoa Bowl
Ingredients:

- 2 cups cooked and shredded Country Captain Chicken
- 2 cups cooked quinoa

- 1 cup kale, chopped
- 1 cup cherry tomatoes, halved
- 1/4 cup pumpkin seeds
- Lemon-tahini dressing (lemon juice, tahini, garlic, salt)

Instructions:

1. In a bowl, combine shredded Country Captain Chicken, cooked quinoa, chopped kale, cherry tomatoes, and pumpkin seeds.
2. Drizzle with lemon-tahini dressing before serving.

14.5 Dairy-Free Country Captain Chicken Cauliflower Wrap

Ingredients:

- 2 cups cooked and shredded Country Captain Chicken
- Large whole wheat or gluten-free wraps
- 1 cup cauliflower florets, roasted
- 1/2 cup hummus
- 1/4 cup sun-dried tomatoes, chopped
- Fresh parsley for garnish

Instructions:

1. Fill each wrap with shredded Country Captain Chicken, roasted cauliflower, hummus, and chopped sun-dried tomatoes.
2. Garnish with fresh parsley before serving.

These healthy twists on Country Captain Chicken offer light and nutritious alternatives, incorporating wholesome ingredients and catering to various dietary preferences. Whether you're opting for a grilled chicken salad, lettuce wraps, cauliflower rice bowls, quinoa creations, or dairy-free wraps, these recipes provide delicious and health-conscious options for enjoying this classic dish.

Chapter 15: Culinary Tips and Tricks

In this chapter, we'll explore a collection of kitchen hacks and cooking techniques to enhance your experience with Country Captain Chicken and elevate your culinary skills.

15.1 The Perfect Chicken Shred

Achieving perfectly shredded chicken for your Country Captain dishes can be made easier with this kitchen hack.

Kitchen Hack:

Place cooked and slightly cooled chicken in a stand mixer. Using the paddle attachment, turn the mixer on low for a few seconds. The chicken will shred beautifully without the need for manual effort.

15.2 Flavor-Infused Oils

Enhance the depth of flavor in your Country Captain Chicken by creating your own infused oils.

Cooking Technique:

In a small saucepan, gently heat olive oil with aromatics such as garlic, ginger, and whole spices like cumin or coriander seeds. Let the flavors infuse over low heat for 10-15 minutes. Strain the oil and use it in your Country Captain Chicken recipes for an extra layer of taste.

15.3 Citrus Zest Enhancement

Give your dishes a burst of freshness by mastering the technique of extracting citrus zest.

Kitchen Hack:

Use a micro plane grater to easily extract the zest from lemons, limes, or oranges. The fine texture ensures that you capture only the flavorful outer layer of the citrus fruit, avoiding the bitter pith.

15.4 Oven-Roasted Spices

Bring out the aromatic qualities of your spices by giving them a quick toast in the oven.

Cooking Technique:

Spread whole spices (such as cumin seeds, coriander seeds, or cardamom pods) on a baking sheet and roast in a preheated oven at 350°F (175°C) for 5-7 minutes. Be cautious not to burn them. Once toasted, grind the spices for a more intense and complex flavor in your Country Captain Chicken spice blend.

15.5 Slow-Cooked Intensity

For a richer and more intense flavor profile in your Country Captain Chicken, consider using a slow-cooking method.

Cooking Technique:

Utilize a slow cooker or crockpot to simmer the ingredients over a longer period. This method allows the flavors to meld and intensify, resulting in a dish with deep and complex tastes.

15.6 Brine for Moisture

Keep your chicken moist and flavorful by incorporating a brining step into your preparation.

Kitchen Hack:

Create a simple brine solution by dissolving salt and sugar in water. Submerge the chicken in the brine for 1-2 hours before cooking. This enhances the chicken's moisture retention and adds a subtle seasoning to the meat.

15.7 Quick Marinades

Infuse your chicken with bold flavors using quick and effective marinades.

Kitchen Hack:

Create a speedy marinade by combining ingredients like yogurt, lemon juice, and your favorite spices. Coat the chicken and let it marinate for at least 30 minutes before cooking. This imparts flavor and tenderness to the meat in a short amount of time.

15.8 Flavorful Rice Tips

Take your rice accompaniments to the next level with these rice-cooking tips.

Cooking Technique:

For a fragrant rice experience, cook it with a cinnamon stick, whole cardamom pods, or a bay leaf. These aromatics infuse the rice with subtle flavors that complement the Country Captain Chicken.

15.9 All-in-One Sheet Pan

Simplify your cooking process and reduce cleanup by utilizing a sheet pan for an all-in-one meal.

Kitchen Hack:

Arrange seasoned chicken and vegetables on a sheet pan, then roast or bake in the oven. This technique not only streamlines the cooking process but also allows the flavors to mingle for a cohesive and delicious outcome.

15.10 Fresh Herb Finishing

Elevate the freshness of your Country Captain Chicken just before serving.

Kitchen Hack:

Sprinkle freshly chopped herbs like cilantro, parsley, or mint over the finished dish. The vibrant colors and aromatic essence will add a burst of brightness to your culinary creation.

Incorporate these kitchen hacks and cooking techniques into your Country Captain Chicken repertoire to enhance flavors, streamline processes, and take your culinary skills to the next level. Whether you're a seasoned chef or a home cook, these tips and tricks are designed to make your cooking experience more enjoyable and the final results even more delicious.

Chapter 16: Traditional Breads and Accompaniments

In this chapter, we'll explore a variety of traditional bread recipes from around the world that perfectly complement the rich flavors of Country Captain Chicken. Additionally, we'll provide some delightful complementary sides to complete your dining experience.

16.1 Naan Bread
Ingredients:

- 4 cups all-purpose flour
- 1 teaspoon baking powder
- 1 teaspoon sugar
- 1/4 teaspoon baking soda
- 1/2 teaspoon salt
- 1 cup plain yogurt
- 1/4 cup milk
- 1 egg, beaten
- 2 tablespoons ghee or melted butter

Instructions:

1. In a large bowl, whisk together flour, baking powder, sugar, baking soda, and salt.
2. In a separate bowl, combine yogurt, milk, and beaten egg.
3. Add the wet ingredients to the dry ingredients and mix until a dough forms.
4. Knead the dough on a floured surface until smooth.
5. Place the dough in a greased bowl, cover with a damp cloth, and let it rise for 1-2 hours.
6. Preheat a skillet over medium-high heat.
7. Divide the dough into golf ball-sized portions and roll each into

a thin oval shape.

8. Cook each naan for 1-2 minutes on each side until puffed and lightly browned.
9. Brush with ghee or melted butter before serving.

16.2 Roti
Ingredients:

- 2 cups whole wheat flour
- 3/4 cup water (approx.)
- 1/2 teaspoon salt

Instructions:

1. In a large bowl, combine whole wheat flour and salt.
2. Gradually add water and knead to form a smooth dough.
3. Divide the dough into golf ball-sized portions.
4. Roll each ball into a thin, round disc.
5. Cook each roti on a hot griddle for about 1-2 minutes on each side or until it puffs up.
6. Serve warm.

16.3 French Baguette
Ingredients:

- 4 cups bread flour
- 2 teaspoons active dry yeast
- 1 1/2 teaspoons salt
- 1 1/2 cups warm water

Instructions:

1. In a large bowl, combine bread flour, active dry yeast, and salt.

2. Gradually add warm water and knead until a smooth dough forms.
3. Place the dough in a greased bowl, cover with a damp cloth, and let it rise for 1-2 hours.
4. Preheat the oven to 450°F (230°C).
5. Punch down the dough and shape it into a baguette.
6. Place the baguette on a baking sheet and let it rise for an additional 30 minutes.
7. Make diagonal slashes on the top of the baguette with a sharp knife.
8. Bake for 20-25 minutes or until golden brown.

16.4 Basmati Rice
Ingredients:

- 2 cups basmati rice
- 4 cups water
- 1 teaspoon salt

Instructions:

1. Rinse the basmati rice under cold water until the water runs clear.
2. In a pot, bring 4 cups of water to a boil.
3. Add the rinsed rice and salt to the boiling water.
4. Reduce heat, cover, and simmer for 15-20 minutes or until the rice is cooked.
5. Fluff the rice with a fork before serving.

16.5 Raita
Ingredients:

- 1 cup Greek yogurt
- 1/2 cucumber, grated

- 1/2 cup mint leaves, chopped
- 1/2 teaspoon cumin powder
- Salt to taste

Instructions:

1. In a bowl, combine Greek yogurt, grated cucumber, chopped mint leaves, cumin powder, and salt.
2. Mix well and refrigerate before serving.

16.6 Mango Chutney
Ingredients:

- 2 ripe mangoes, peeled and diced
- 1/4 cup red onion, finely chopped
- 1/4 cup cilantro, chopped
- 1 tablespoon lime juice
- 1 teaspoon grated ginger
- 1/2 teaspoon red pepper flakes
- Salt to taste

Instructions:

1. In a bowl, combine diced mangoes, chopped red onion, cilantro, lime juice, grated ginger, red pepper flakes, and salt.
2. Mix well and refrigerate before serving.

These traditional breads and accompaniments provide a diverse array of flavors and textures to complement your Country Captain Chicken. From the soft and pillowy naan to the crusty French baguette, each bread is paired with delightful sides like raita and mango chutney, creating a well-rounded and satisfying meal.

Chapter 17: Sensational Sauces: Dips, Dressings, and Condiments

In this chapter, we'll dive into the world of sensational sauces, featuring homemade condiments and creative dips that elevate the flavors of your Country Captain Chicken dishes.

17.1 Spiced Tomato Chutney

Ingredients:

- 2 cups tomatoes, diced
- 1/2 cup red onion, finely chopped
- 1/4 cup brown sugar
- 1/4 cup apple cider vinegar
- 1 teaspoon mustard seeds
- 1 teaspoon cumin seeds
- 1/2 teaspoon red pepper flakes
- Salt to taste

Instructions:

1. In a saucepan, combine tomatoes, red onion, brown sugar, apple cider vinegar, mustard seeds, cumin seeds, red pepper flakes, and salt.
2. Bring to a simmer over medium heat.
3. Cook, stirring occasionally, until the chutney thickens and the tomatoes break down.
4. Let it cool before serving.

17.2 Cilantro Mint Yogurt Sauce

Ingredients:

- 1 cup Greek yogurt
- 1/4 cup fresh cilantro, chopped

- 1/4 cup fresh mint, chopped
- 1 tablespoon lime juice
- 1 teaspoon honey
- Salt and pepper to taste

Instructions:

1. In a bowl, whisk together Greek yogurt, chopped cilantro, chopped mint, lime juice, honey, salt, and pepper.
2. Adjust the seasoning to taste.
3. Refrigerate before serving.

17.3 Tangy Tamarind Dip
Ingredients:

- 1/2 cup tamarind paste
- 1/4 cup honey
- 2 tablespoons soy sauce
- 1 tablespoon rice vinegar
- 1 teaspoon grated ginger
- 1/2 teaspoon garlic powder
- 1/4 teaspoon red pepper flakes

Instructions:

1. In a bowl, combine tamarind paste, honey, soy sauce, rice vinegar, grated ginger, garlic powder, and red pepper flakes.
2. Whisk until well combined.
3. Refrigerate before serving.

17.4 Garlic Sesame Aioli
Ingredients:

- 1/2 cup mayonnaise

- 1 tablespoon sesame oil
- 1 tablespoon soy sauce
- 1 clove garlic, minced
- 1 teaspoon lemon juice
- Salt and pepper to taste

Instructions:

1. In a bowl, mix together mayonnaise, sesame oil, soy sauce, minced garlic, lemon juice, salt, and pepper.
2. Adjust the seasoning to taste.
3. Refrigerate before serving.

17.5 Roasted Red Pepper Hummus
Ingredients:

- 1 can (15 oz) chickpeas, drained and rinsed
- 1/2 cup roasted red peppers, drained
- 1/4 cup tahini
- 2 tablespoons olive oil
- 2 tablespoons lemon juice
- 1 clove garlic, minced
- 1/2 teaspoon cumin
- Salt and pepper to taste

Instructions:

1. In a food processor, combine chickpeas, roasted red peppers, tahini, olive oil, lemon juice, minced garlic, cumin, salt, and pepper.
2. Blend until smooth.
3. Refrigerate before serving.

17.6 Mango Salsa

Ingredients:

- 1 ripe mango, diced
- 1/2 red onion, finely chopped
- 1/4 cup fresh cilantro, chopped
- 1 jalapeño, seeded and finely chopped
- Juice of 1 lime
- Salt and pepper to taste

Instructions:

1. In a bowl, combine diced mango, chopped red onion, chopped cilantro, chopped jalapeño, lime juice, salt, and pepper.
2. Mix well.
3. Refrigerate before serving.

These sensational sauces, dips, and condiments add a burst of flavor and creativity to your Country Captain Chicken dishes. From the spiced tomato chutney to the mango salsa, each homemade creation is designed to enhance and complement the rich and aromatic flavors of your culinary masterpiece. Explore these delightful accompaniments and elevate your dining experience with these sensational sauces.

Chapter 18: Desserts with a Chicken Twist

In this unique chapter, we'll explore delightful desserts with a surprising chicken twist, offering sweet endings to your savory meals. These inventive recipes showcase the versatility of chicken, turning it into a surprising and delicious ingredient for indulgent treats.

18.1 Country Captain Chicken Empanadas

Ingredients:

Dough:

- 2 cups all-purpose flour
- 1/2 cup unsalted butter, cold and cubed
- 1/2 cup cold water
- 1/2 teaspoon salt

Filling:

- 1 cup cooked and shredded Country Captain Chicken
- 1/2 cup dried apricots, chopped
- 1/4 cup brown sugar
- 1/4 cup almonds, chopped
- 1/2 teaspoon cinnamon
- 1/4 teaspoon nutmeg
- Egg wash (1 egg beaten with 1 tablespoon water)

Instructions:

Dough:

1. In a food processor, combine flour, cold butter, and salt. Pulse until it resembles coarse crumbs.
2. With the processor running, slowly add cold water until the dough comes together.

3. Turn the dough out onto a floured surface, knead briefly, then wrap in plastic wrap and refrigerate for at least 30 minutes.

Filling:

1. In a bowl, mix shredded Country Captain Chicken, chopped dried apricots, brown sugar, chopped almonds, cinnamon, and nutmeg.

Assembly:

1. Preheat the oven to 375°F (190°C).
2. Roll out the chilled dough and cut circles.
3. Place a spoonful of the chicken filling in the center of each circle.
4. Fold the dough over the filling, creating a half-moon shape, and press the edges to seal.
5. Brush each empanada with the egg wash.
6. Bake for 15-20 minutes or until golden brown.

18.2 Curry Chicken Ice Cream
Ingredients:

- 2 cups heavy cream
- 1 cup whole milk
- 3/4 cup granulated sugar
- 1 tablespoon curry powder
- 1/2 teaspoon turmeric
- 1 cup cooked and pureed Country Captain Chicken

Instructions:

1. In a saucepan over medium heat, combine heavy cream, whole

milk, granulated sugar, curry powder, and turmeric.

2. Heat the mixture until it starts to steam, but do not boil.

3. Remove from heat and let it cool to room temperature.

4. Once cooled, stir in the pureed Country Captain Chicken.

5. Chill the mixture in the refrigerator for at least 4 hours or overnight.

6. Churn the mixture in an ice cream maker according to the manufacturer's

7. instructions.

8. Transfer the churned ice cream to a lidded container and freeze until firm.

18.3 Savory Chicken and Pecan Pie
Ingredients:
Pie Crust:

- 1 1/4 cups all-purpose flour
- 1/2 cup unsalted butter, cold and cubed
- 1/4 teaspoon salt
- 2-3 tablespoons ice water

Filling:

- 2 cups cooked and shredded Country Captain Chicken
- 1 cup pecans, chopped
- 1/2 cup brown sugar
- 1/4 cup maple syrup
- 1/4 cup unsalted butter, melted
- 3 eggs, beaten
- 1 teaspoon vanilla extract
- 1/4 teaspoon salt

Instructions:
Pie Crust:

1. In a food processor, combine flour, cold butter, and salt. Pulse until it resembles coarse crumbs.
2. With the processor running, slowly add ice water until the dough comes together.
3. Turn the dough out onto a floured surface, knead briefly, then wrap in plastic wrap and refrigerate for at least 30 minutes.

Filling:

1. In a bowl, mix shredded Country Captain Chicken, chopped pecans, brown sugar, maple syrup, melted butter, beaten eggs, vanilla extract, and salt.

Assembly:

1. Preheat the oven to 375°F (190°C).
2. Roll out the chilled dough and line a pie dish.
3. Pour the chicken-pecan filling into the pie crust.
4. Bake for 40-45 minutes or until the filling is set and the crust is golden brown.
5. Let it cool before slicing.

18.4 Chicken and Apple Strudel
Ingredients:

- 1 package phyllo dough, thawed
- 1/2 cup unsalted butter, melted
- 2 cups cooked and shredded Country Captain Chicken
- 2 apples, peeled and thinly sliced
- 1/4 cup brown sugar
- 1/2 teaspoon cinnamon
- 1/4 cup breadcrumbs

Instructions:

1. Preheat the oven to 375°F (190°C).
2. Lay out one sheet of phyllo dough and brush it with melted butter. Repeat with 5 more sheets, layering them on top of each other.
3. In a bowl, mix shredded Country Captain Chicken, sliced apples, brown sugar, and cinnamon.
4. Spread breadcrumbs over the buttered phyllo dough, leaving a border around the edges.
5. Spoon the chicken and apple mixture over the breadcrumbs.
6. Fold in the sides of the phyllo and roll it up, creating a strudel.
7. Place the strudel on a baking sheet and brush with more melted butter.
8. Bake for 25-30 minutes or until golden brown.

These inventive desserts with a chicken twist offer a surprising and delightful way to conclude your meals. From the savory empanadas to the unique curry chicken ice cream, each dessert showcases the versatility of Country Captain Chicken in creating memorable and delicious sweet treats. Embrace the unexpected and savor the delightful combination of sweet and savory flavors in these inventive desserts.

Chapter 19: Beverage Pairings

In this chapter, we'll explore perfect drinks to accompany your flavorful Country Captain Chicken dishes. From refreshing beverages to complement the bold spices to delightful cocktails for special occasions, these pairings will enhance your dining experience.

19.1 Minty Cucumber Lemonade
Ingredients:

- 1 cucumber, peeled and sliced
- 1/4 cup fresh mint leaves
- 1 cup fresh lemon juice
- 1/2 cup simple syrup (equal parts water and sugar, dissolved)
- 4 cups cold water
- Ice cubes

Instructions:

1. In a blender, combine cucumber slices, fresh mint leaves, fresh lemon juice, and simple syrup.
2. Blend until smooth.
3. Strain the mixture into a pitcher to remove solids.
4. Add cold water to the pitcher and stir well.
5. Serve over ice.

19.2 Ginger Peach Iced Tea
Ingredients:

- 4 cups brewed black tea, chilled
- 1 cup peach nectar
- 1/4 cup honey

- 1 tablespoon fresh ginger, grated
- Peach slices and mint for garnish
- Ice cubes

Instructions:

1. In a pitcher, combine chilled black tea, peach nectar, honey, and grated ginger.
2. Stir until the honey is dissolved.
3. Refrigerate for at least 1 hour.
4. Serve over ice and garnish with peach slices and mint.

19.3 Spicy Mango Margarita
Ingredients:

- 2 cups mango nectar
- 1/2 cup tequila
- 1/4 cup triple sec
- 1 jalapeño, sliced
- 1/4 cup fresh lime juice
- Salt for rimming glasses
- Ice cubes·

Instructions:

1. In a blender, combine mango nectar, tequila, triple sec, sliced jalapeño, and fresh lime juice.
2. Blend until smooth.
3. Rim glasses with salt.
4. Fill glasses with ice and pour the mango margarita mixture over the ice.

19.4 Cucumber-Mint Sparkler
Ingredients:

- 1 cucumber, thinly sliced
- 1/4 cup fresh mint leaves
- 1 tablespoon agave syrup
- 2 cups sparkling water
- Ice cubes

Instructions:

1. In a pitcher, muddle cucumber slices, fresh mint leaves, and agave syrup.
2. Add sparkling water to the pitcher and stir gently.
3. Serve over ice.

19.5 Classic Lassi
Ingredients:

- 1 cup plain yogurt
- 1 cup cold water
- 2 tablespoons sugar
- Pinch of ground cardamom
- Ice cubes

Instructions:

1. In a blender, combine plain yogurt, cold water, sugar, and ground cardamom.
2. Blend until smooth.
3. Serve over ice.

19.6 Pineapple Ginger Sparkling Mocktail
Ingredients:

- 2 cups pineapple juice
- 1 tablespoon fresh ginger, grated

- 1 tablespoon honey
- 2 cups sparkling water
- Pineapple slices and mint for garnish
- Ice cubes

Instructions:

1. In a pitcher, combine pineapple juice, grated ginger, and honey.
2. Stir until honey is dissolved.
3. Add sparkling water and stir gently.
4. Serve over ice and garnish with pineapple slices and mint.

Pair these delightful beverages with your Country Captain Chicken creations to enhance the dining experience. Whether you prefer a refreshing minty cucumber lemonade, a spicy mango margarita, or a classic lassi, these drink pairings are designed to complement the rich and aromatic flavors of Country Captain Chicken, creating a well-rounded and satisfying meal. Cheers to a delicious dining experience!

Chapter 20: Celebrating Seasons: Holiday Specials

In this chapter, we'll explore festive recipes for special occasions, perfect for celebrating seasons and creating memorable meals during holidays and gatherings. From appetizers to main courses and desserts, these recipes are designed to bring joy and flavor to your festive occasions.

20.1 Stuffed Acorn Squash with Country Captain Chicken
Ingredients:
Filling:

- 2 acorn squashes, halved and seeds removed
- 2 cups cooked and shredded Country Captain Chicken
- 1 cup quinoa, cooked
- 1/2 cup dried cranberries
- 1/4 cup chopped pecans
- 2 tablespoons maple syrup
- 1 teaspoon cinnamon
- Salt and pepper to taste

Instructions:

1. Preheat the oven to 375°F (190°C).
2. Place acorn squash halves on a baking sheet.
3. In a bowl, mix shredded Country Captain Chicken, cooked quinoa, dried cranberries, chopped pecans, maple syrup, cinnamon, salt, and pepper.
4. Fill each acorn squash half with the chicken and quinoa mixture.
5. Bake for 30-40 minutes or until the squash is tender.

20.2 Cranberry and Walnut Country Captain Chicken Salad
Ingredients:

Salad:

- 4 cups mixed salad greens
- 2 cups cooked and shredded Country Captain Chicken
- 1 cup dried cranberries
- 1/2 cup crumbled feta cheese
- 1/2 cup chopped walnuts

Dressing:

- 1/4 cup olive oil
- 2 tablespoons balsamic vinegar
- 1 tablespoon Dijon mustard
- 1 tablespoon honey
- Salt and pepper to taste

Instructions:

1. In a large bowl, combine mixed salad greens, shredded Country Captain Chicken, dried cranberries, feta cheese, and chopped walnuts.
2. In a small bowl, whisk together olive oil, balsamic vinegar, Dijon mustard, honey, salt, and pepper.
3. Drizzle the dressing over the salad and toss gently before serving.

20.3 Holiday Spice Roast Chicken
Ingredients:
Spice Rub:

- 1 tablespoon paprika
- 1 tablespoon brown sugar
- 1 teaspoon garlic powder
- 1 teaspoon onion powder

- 1/2 teaspoon cinnamon
- 1/2 teaspoon nutmeg
- 1/2 teaspoon salt
- 1/4 teaspoon black pepper

Roast Chicken:

- 1 whole chicken (about 4-5 pounds)
- 2 tablespoons olive oil
- 1 orange, quartered
- 1 onion, quartered
- Fresh rosemary sprigs

Instructions:

1. Preheat the oven to 375°F (190°C).
2. In a small bowl, mix together all the spices for the rub.
3. Rub the spice mixture all over the chicken, including under the skin.
4. Place the chicken in a roasting pan.
5. Drizzle olive oil over the chicken.
6. Stuff the cavity with orange quarters, onion quarters, and fresh rosemary.
7. Roast for about 1.5 to 2 hours or until the internal temperature reaches 165°F (74°C).

20.4 Pecan Pie Cheesecake with Caramel Drizzle
Ingredients:
Crust:

- 1 1/2 cups graham cracker crumbs
- 1/2 cup melted butter

- 1/4 cup granulated sugar

Cheesecake Filling:

- 4 packages (8 oz each) cream cheese, softened
- 1 1/4 cups brown sugar
- 1/2 cup granulated sugar
- 4 large eggs
- 1/4 cup all-purpose flour
- 1 teaspoon vanilla extract

Pecan Pie Topping:

- 1 cup pecan halves
- 1/2 cup light corn syrup
- 1/4 cup brown sugar
- 2 tablespoons melted butter
- 1 teaspoon vanilla extract

Caramel Drizzle:

- 1/2 cup caramel sauce

Instructions:

1. Preheat the oven to 325°F (163°C). Grease a 9-inch springform pan.
2. In a bowl, mix graham cracker crumbs, melted butter, and granulated sugar. Press the mixture into the bottom of the prepared pan.
3. In a large bowl, beat cream cheese until smooth. Add brown sugar and granulated sugar, beating until well combined.
4. Add eggs one at a time, beating well after each addition. Stir in flour and vanilla extract.

5. Pour the cream cheese mixture over the crust in the pan.

6. In a separate bowl, mix pecan halves, corn syrup, brown sugar, melted butter, and vanilla extract for the pecan pie topping. Spoon this mixture over the cream cheese layer.

7. Bake for about 1 hour or until the center is set.

8. Let the cheesecake cool to room temperature, then refrigerate for at least 4 hours or overnight.

9. Drizzle caramel sauce over the chilled cheesecake before serving.

The "Country Captain Chicken Cookbook" takes you on a culinary journey through a diverse array of recipes, exploring the rich and aromatic flavors of Country Captain Chicken. From classic preparations to creative twists and innovative pairings, this cookbook is a celebration of the versatility of this beloved dish.

In this cookbook, you've discovered a range of recipes spanning appetizers, main courses, side dishes, desserts, and even unique beverage pairings. The chapters guide you through the essentials of preparing and cooking Country Captain Chicken, exploring regional variations, mastering the art of marination, perfecting rice accompaniments, and even venturing into unexpected territories with desserts featuring a chicken twist.

The cookbook also recognizes the importance of complementing the main dish with delightful sides, sauces, and beverages. Whether you're exploring the refreshing Minty Cucumber Lemonade, the spicy Mango Margarita, or the hearty Stuffed Acorn Squash with Country Captain Chicken, each recipe is crafted to enhance your culinary experience.

During special occasions and holiday celebrations, the "Celebrating Seasons: Holiday Specials" chapter provides you with festive recipes to create memorable meals. From the Holiday Spice Roast Chicken to the indulgent Pecan Pie Cheesecake with Caramel Drizzle, these recipes are designed to bring warmth and joy to your gatherings.

In the "Beverage Pairings" chapter, you've found the perfect drinks to accompany Country Captain Chicken, ranging from classic lassi to inventive cocktails like the Cucumber-Mint Sparkler. These pairings are crafted to balance and enhance the flavors of your meals.

This cookbook is not just a collection of recipes but an invitation to embark on a culinary adventure. Whether you're a seasoned chef or an enthusiastic home cook, these recipes provide an opportunity to explore, experiment, and savor the delightful world of Country Captain Chicken in all its delicious forms.

Thank you for joining us on this gastronomic journey. May your kitchen be filled with the enticing aromas and flavors of Country Captain Chicken, creating moments of joy and satisfaction at your table. Happy cooking!

www.ingramcontent.com/pod-product-compliance
Lightning Source LLC
Chambersburg PA
CBHW051249160726
47994CB00003B/1093